Spiritual Journey
Of
An American Muslim

Sabur Abdul-Salaam

Spiritual Journey Of An American Muslim
By Sabur Abdul-Salaam

All praise is due to Allah the Lord of the Worlds and may His peace and blessings be on His Noble Messenger Muhammad, and on his family and his companions and the believers

This book is dedicated to my mother who always made it her top priority to be a good wife to her husband and a good mother to her children, and my two sons Yusuf and Osama who always inspired me to be conscious of the example that I was setting.

May Allah bless them with Jennat Al Firdous

Contents

Chapter 6

Chapter 7

Acknowledgment

I want to acknowledge the support of my ex-wife Ferdous, who for twenty-six years encouraged me to write this book, but Allah decreed that the book would not be written until after our divorce, and my brother Wakil who joined me in faith many years ago. And my youngest brother Jimmy, even though we haven't spent that much time together, we have always been in each others prayers. And my oldest sister Ella whose home has always been my home away from home, and my other sisters: Francine, Lorraine, Gail, Barbara and Lynette, who I always knew were there for me if I ever needed them. And my very good friend Shaikh Khalil Abdulkhabir who very generously consented to do the book's layout and to use his artistic skills to do the book's cover.

I also have to include Shaikh Ahmad Kobeisey who has been my neighbor, friend and religious advisor for years. And finally, my Shaikh, Safa Al Shiraida, who was a role model for me in my early days as a Muslim, and who has always exemplified those words of the Prophet (pbuh), "An action is nothing but its intention, and he whose migration is for Allah and His Messenger, his migration is for Allah and His Messenger."

May Allah bless, guide and have mercy on everyone I have mentioned, and the many Muslims who I have not mentioned but have been a tremendous help to me during my spiritual journey. May Allah forgive our sins and bless us with Jennat Al Firdous.

Preface

Neither my parents nor my older brother had graduated from high school, so I was the first to graduate because my mother expected me to. In spite of the fact that I did not like school and was not a good student, my family members and some others always thought that I was smart. Having a large family, eventually having three brothers and six sisters, obviously money was tight in my lower middle-class home. Wanting to be independent and not a burden on my family was always more important than my going to school.

After graduating from high school, I never considered going to college, but instead I joined the army. After three years, in 1968, I was honorably discharged in the thick of the Civil Rights/Black Power movement era. I was not culturally or politically conscious at that point in my life until a friend gave me a copy of "The Autobiography of Malcolm X" and told me that I had to read it. You might say that Malcolm's autobiography elevated me culturally, politically and spiritually, and I began reading books about black people.

A year or two later, after having moved from Philadelphia back to New York City, I woke up around 2 AM one morning and wrote a poem. I don't remember ever having written a poem before except for a high school English assignment. However, during the next few years I would write quite a few poems and eventually publish a book of poems under a different name. I used to also read my poems at different social and cultural events in New

York City and Newark, New Jersey. It was at these events that I began having contact with American Sunni Muslims which culminated in my eventually converting to Islam.

It was the Religion of Islam that gave me an appreciation for knowledge and motivated me, at 29 years of age, to go to college. It was in college that I eventually realized exactly how much I enjoyed writing. For years, in spite of my enjoyment of writing, I never really seriously considered writing a book. Because of my reverence for knowledge I thought it best to leave the writing of books to the Islamic scholars. To me it was very important, that if I wrote a book, I would either want it to help Muslims in their practice of Islam or help guide non-Muslims to Islam. So the deterrent for me, and probably rightly so, was that the Muslim scholars were better able to help Muslims with their practice and/or guide non-Muslims to Islam.

Eight years ago I retired from my Muslim Chaplain's position with the New York State Department of Correctional Services, which meant that I had more time for reflection and introspection. It was during that time that I became painfully aware of a very serious problem within the American Muslim community. Even though Islam strongly emphasizes "brotherhood", in my opinion, the division between different Muslim ethnic groups has seriously increased during the past three decades.

On a personal level, I have truly experienced the universal brotherhood that Malik Shabazz (Malcolm X) observed when he made his pilgrimage to Mecca. I know brothers from many different countries, who I could not love more even if they were my biological brothers. However, when it comes to mosques in towns and cities, and national organizations, there is often a serious need for improvement.

In the 1960's, the Black Panther leader Eldridge Cleaver (whose son converted to Islam and is now working on a Ph D in Islamic Studies) said, "if you are not part of the solution you are part of the problem", and I took that to heart. During the past 30 years I have tried to work with all Muslims but my very limited success has been a source of frustration and has jaded me.

Alex Haley, through his book "Roots" which was made into a television mini-series, made a tremendous contribution to American Society by sharing his family's history. White Americans learned about slavery and the Black American experience. And Black Americans also learned about slavery and that some of their ancestors were Muslims. Malik Shabazz, more commonly known as Malcolm X, through his autobiography, also made a tremendous contribution to American Society by showing the other side of the Black experience. Alex Haley's family history and his upward mobility exemplified the American Dream, while Malcolm's family history and his assassination, exemplified the American Nightmare. However, it also showed the universal brotherhood he had witnessed in Mecca, after he had converted to Islam. His book introduced many Americans to Islam, and many of us eventually embraced the faith.

In 2011 I read a good book, "The Dar Ul Islam Movement (An American Odyssey Revisited) by Shaikh Mahmoud Ibrahim, a brother from New York City who I actually know and the opening chapter is his brief autobiography and his relationship with the Dar Ul Islam Movement. After reading his book and the encouragement of my good friend Khalil Abdulkhabir (who also did the cover layout for this book), I decided that maybe my story was worth telling. It is another small piece of the puzzle that shows Islam and the Muslims in America. It may help my brothers who were born in other countries, have a better understanding of their African American brothers, because some people believe that you can't understand someone until you have walked a mile in their shoes, so my book will allow people to walk in my shoes. Or if my book helps to guide just one person to the religion of Islam, my efforts will not have been in vain.

In a final note, I am not saying that my life experiences and observations is an accurate representation of all American Muslim men. My good friend Dr. Ihsan Bagby, who did his undergraduate studies at the very prestigious Obelin College and went on to earn a Ph D in Islamic Studies, obviously some aspects of his life were very different from mine, but I also feel confident that he would tell you that he could relate to many of my experiences, Insha Allah.

Sabur Abdul-Salaam
February 29, 2012

Foreword

I chose "Spiritual Journey of An American Muslim" as the title of my book because the title should tell you something about the content of a book, and the "Oxford Dictionary of Current English" defines "spiritual" as 1. of the spirit or soul, 2. religious, divine, inspired. So my book describes how God guided the journey of my soul from my birth too my Shahadah, the moment I embraced the religion of Islam.

This book is not a detailed description of my religious life as a Christian, even though I do touch on certain aspects. Nor is it a detailed description of the beliefs and practices of the religion of Islam, even though I do mention some Islamic practices and concepts. It is my spiritual journey.

Some Muslims may consider some aspects of my book as being crude, but remember this is my life before I became a Muslim. Some of the Prophet Muhammad's, peace and blessings be upon him (pbuh), companions lead crude lives before they converted to Islam. Drinking wine, gambling, and sexually promiscuous behavior, were common practices in Mecca, at the time Muhammad (pbuh) received his prophethood.

Lastly, I have included a glossary because there are some slang expressions from the 1960's and 1970's that I used in my pre-shahadah poetry that may need to be defined. And there are some Islamic words or terms that may also need to be defined. All that having been said, now let's begin.

Chapter 1

My Early Years

My Birth and First Hijrah

Some months before I was born, my mother packed some of her and my older brother Sonny's things and boarded a train in New York City, bound for South Carolina. I was conceived in New York City but was destined to be born in South Carolina. My mother was going to her father's house for the sole purpose of giving birth to me. Twenty-seven years later I would convert to Islam and choose the first name Sabur which is an Arabic word meaning "patience", because patience is a virtue that I always admired and desperately needed. Even then I had so little patience that I didn't even wait for the mid-wife who was supposed to deliver me. By the time she arrived I was already waiting for her so all she did was to clean me up. So on October 9, 1946, in my grandfather's house in a small town in South Carolina I came into this world and my spiritual journey began.

A few months later my mother would again pack our belongings and board a train to go back to New York City, but we were not going to my father's home, my mother and brother, would never live with my father again. He was in between wars, he had been drafted in World War II and would be drafted again in the Korean War, but at that time he was busy nurturing his career as a tap dancer and theat-

1

rical promoter. So we were instead going to my mother's aunt and uncle's home in the Bronx where I would live for the next twelve years.

Both my mother's aunt and uncle were born in 1891 and was living in Georgia before they moved north eventually settling in the Bronx. During World War I they needed cheap laborers in the north so there were trains that would take Black men from the southern states to the northern states for free. So my mother's uncle went to New Jersey first and then settled in New York City and sent for his wife. There home became the transitional residence for many of their nieces and nephews when they moved to New York. They would live with them until they found work and was able to get a place of their own.

My mother's uncle was a "Jack of all trades", he could do electrical work, plumbing and carpentry but being Black, of course he could not get in any of those unions. So he worked as a superintendent of an apartment building, and had the basement apartment and maintained the other fifty apartments which were only rented to White people. On television I would see Black men who would always look at the ground and say "yessa boss" but that was not my uncle. Part of my uncle's responsibilities was to collect the rent from the tenants.

In our living room we had a desk where a big receipt book was kept. And when tenants would come to pay the rent with either a check or cash, my uncle would give them a receipt. Because my uncle was paid a very meager salary he would often find himself in need of some money before payday, so he would just give himself an advance from the rent money.

When the Jewish landlord would come to collect the rent money and check it against the receipts he would say "Joe the cash is short", but knowing that he was underpaid and that his electrical, plumbing and carpentry skills were saving the landlord tons of money, so my mother's uncle would just curse him out and say "deduct it from my pay" and that would be that until the next time. My mother's uncle was a good man and I called him Dad until the day he died because he was my "defacto father" for the first twelve years of my life.

You may want to earmark this page because I know this is going to be confusing, but from this point on when I refer to my biological mother or father, I will call them my mother or father, but when I refer to my mother's Aunt Edith or her Uncle Joe, who I lived with in the Bronx the first twelve years of my life, I will call them mom and dad.

My Mother, Stepfather, Younger Siblings and my Jewish friend.

The introduction to my mother's obituary, very beautifully summarizes her life, in the following way:

Ella Johnson Whitaker Freeland was born to Arthur and Rosa Johnson on April 8, 1927 in Beaufort, South Carolina. Ella was one of six siblings, Levi, Willie, Arthur, Eva and Edith who preceded her in death. Ella was educated in South Carolina's public school system. She left South Carolina in 1942 and moved to New York where she resided with her aunt and uncle, Joseph and Edith Johnson. Ella worked various positions in New York City until she met and married The Rev. Albert C. Whitaker, Sr., on June 24, 1951. She relocated to Philadelphia, PA where she has resided for the past 55 years.

Ella worked very hard at an early age and once she married, her work in life was to be a good wife, mother and caring friend to anyone that needed her. When her husband of 24 years passed away suddenly on June 29, 1975, Ella went on to raise her five youngest children on her own. She had the beauty of Cleopatra, the strength of a lioness, the gentleness of a lamb and the determination of a one woman army.

So it was my mother's aunt and uncle, my older brother, me and my cousin Edie, who was more like an older sister, living together in the Bronx when my mother remarried and moved to Philadelphia to live with her new husband and his two sons Albert Jr. and Curly. I was four years old at the time but it was decided that Sonny and I would continue to live in New York at least for a while.

My mother remarrying and moving to Philadelphia made me and my brother Sonny even closer than we had been before. Remember my dad was in his middle fifties' when I was born so he didn't teach Sonny and I how to ride a bike or play ball the way many dads do, so ever since I could remember, Sonny and I did a lot of things together. On one occasion Sonny took me to the Bronx Zoo and while we were there he spent our carfare buying us something to eat and then he carried me all the way home on his back. On another occasion, knowing how much I loved French Fries, Sonny took me to a diner and he only had enough money for one order so we sat there and ate that one order together. When we finished the French Fries, the storeowner who was probably Irish, because of the way we shared the food, he gave us a second order for free. I was as happy as a kid in a candy factory.

Two years later my brother Wakil (he chose that name when he converted to Islam) was born, he was the first of the eight children my mother and stepfather would have: Ella, Francine, Lorraine, Gail, Jimmy, Barbara and Lynette would come during the following twelve years.

In spite of the fact my mother treated all of her children as though they were an only child, I have one distinction that can not be claimed by any of my other siblings. I was the only child my mother breast fed. Some of my siblings used to say I was my mother's favorite, which may or may not have been true but my mother and I was always very close, and may be that was why, during her last hospital stay before she died, she declared, "There is only One God and Muhammad is the Messenger of God".

There is a verse in the Quran that says, "With difficulty goes ease". This life is a test, but because of Allah's mercy, he never makes the test to difficult, consequently, with every difficulty He provides some ease.

I remember the day my mother married my stepfather and then the following morning I woke up and was told they were in Philadelphia. To a young child, who at that time had no memory of his father, and then with my mother's absence, I could have been emotionally devastated. Sonny and I was very close but he was already in school and had his own friends so there was only a limited amount of time that we could be together. But as Allah would have it, a Jewish family moved into a first floor apartment and they had one child, a boy a year younger than I was.

I began spending more time in their apartment than I did in mine. As far as the mother was concerned, I couldn't wear out my welcome. The boy (we can call him David) was a spoiled brat, so by him having a playmate helped his mother maintain her sanity. Actually, it was a blessing for all of us, David and I would play with his many toys or watch cartoons on television (his family bought a TV a year or two before mine), freeing his mother to do whatever else she needed to do. I also would eat there regularly, which I thoroughly enjoyed because his mother was an excellent cook.

I remember when the movie the "Ten Commandments" was released. David's mother took him and I too see it. Because the movie was very long, they showed half and then had an intermission. David's mother had packed sandwiches, so during the intermission we ate the sandwiches and then saw the rest of the movie. However, it was during the intermission that I noticed that all the other children in the movie were white (and probably the majority were Jewish) but David's family always treated me like I was one of the family so I didn't feel uncomfortable at all.

David had always been a sickly child so his mother would only allow him to go outside for some fresh air for maybe a half-hour a day if the weather was nice. My spending so much time in David's house was fine for a couple of years but once I started school my circle of friends increased and I became more conscious of the differences between the student population: racial/ethnic, Blacks, Whites, Hispanics etc., as well as social, economic and intellectual differences (those young people who are called "nerds" today were called "bookworms" when I was a child).

With the passing of each year I found myself spending less and less time with David and more time with other friends. Eventually it reached the point where I would just stop by occasionally to see how he was doing. Then one day they sprang a surprise on me, David's parents had gotten him a puppy and they proudly informed me, expecting me to take it as a compliment, they had named the puppy after me. I smiled but I really took it as an insult, it was as though they were replacing one pet with another pet. But be that what it may, that one compliment/insult did not erase all the kindness and generosity they had showed me during the previous few years and may be that was why I rejected the racist rhetoric of the Nation of Islam when I was confronted with it years later in Philadelphia. When they said that all White people were devils, I knew from personal experiences, that was not true.

God, Me and the Christianity

In spite of the fact, that dad would curse people out when they made him angry, he was a God fearing and religious man. He would go to church every Sunday, bless the food before eating and mom said he would say his prayers before going to bed every night. Spiritually he was a good

6

role model for me because up until the age of nineteen, I had a strong belief in God and said my prayers, before going to bed, every night.

Dad even sang on the church choir, and when I could not have been more than three years old, he would take me to church with him and some of my earliest memories were of me sitting up in the choir section with him and I would move my mouth pretending to sing the song that the choir was singing. That was fun but the best part of going to church was the sweet potato pie they sold in the basement after the church service was over.

When I was a few years older, my brother Sonny and I would go to Sunday school at the Lutheran church that was a cross the street from the apartment building where we lived. We did that for maybe a year and then Sonny realized that instead of going to Sunday school, we could take the money that we were given to put in the collection plate and go to the corner bakery, buy some cupcakes and go to the neighborhood park instead.

It was also around this time that I started kindergarten at P.S. 28 on Tremont Avenue. The majority of the students were White with some Blacks and even less Hispanics. Even though I was a skinny little kid, in that White neighborhood, many of the young White boys thought that all Black boys were tough. Their thinking that I was tough was fine with me because being tough does have some perks but it almost got me killed.

God Was Always Protecting Me

I had a lot of relatives in the south because my mother's Aunt Edith was from South Carolina but Aunt Edith's husband, Uncle Joe, was from Georgia. So ever since I could remember, we would spend some time during the summers either in Georgia or South Carolina. One summer when I was around seven or eight years old, we were visiting Georgia and riding in my dad's car, we drove by a white boy around my age who called us niggers. It seemed like we had only drove a few blocks when we came to one of my relative's home and stopped. As I said before, in my neighborhood in the Bronx, most white boys considered black boys tough, so obviously I was not used to having a white boy call me a nigger.

So when we got out of the car I very quietly slipped away and went looking for that white boy. I walked for blocks and couldn't find him, thank God! Remember this was the early 1950's and I hate to think what white men would have done to a black boy from New York City, who beat up a white boy. If there is any doubt in your mind as to what would have happened, just remember Emmett Till.

Emmett Louis Till...was an African-American boy who was brutally murdered in Mississippi at the age of 14 after reportedly flirting with a white woman. Till was from Chicago, Illinois, visiting his relatives in the Mississippi Delta region when he spoke to 21-year-old Carolyn Bryant, the married proprietor of a small grocery store. Several nights later, Bryant's husband Roy and his half-brother J. W. Milam arrived at Till's great-uncle's house where they took Till, transported him to a barn, beat him and gouged out one of his eyes, before shooting him through the head and disposing of his body in the Tallahatchie River, weighting it with a 70-pound cotton gin fan tied around his neck with barbed wire. His body was discovered and retrieved from the river three days later. (Excerpt from Wikipedia, the free encyclopedia)

If not for God's mercy and protection, my spiritual journey may not have ever been completed.

My Father and His Side of the Family

My paternal grandfather, Thomas Phillips, traveled from Georgia on the same train with my mother's Uncle Joe and they became lifelong friends. They both initially settled in Newark, New Jersey, and my father, Julius Andrew Phillips (aka "Buddy Phillips") was born in Newark, on May 6, 1923.

My paternal grandfather's visits to see his old friend, my dad, are the first memories that I have of any one from my father's side of the family. I liked Grandpa Thomas very much, he would always give me money and it was obvious that he loved me. Him and my paternal grandmother were either separated or divorced by that time and it would be a couple of years before I would meet my paternal grandmother. They were the only two grandparents that I had, my maternal grandmother died when my mother was a young girl and my maternal grandfather died when I was a baby.

One day I came home from school just before the Christmas vacation, I think I was in the first grade at the time, and I found and old lady and a young lady in my home. I was told that the old lady was my grandmother and the young lady was her granddaughter my cousin Jean. They had some packages but they also had a child's book bag which was not wrapped up or in a bag. I told my grandmother I need a book bag like that for school. She said I could not have that one but if I asked Santa Claus, maybe he would give me one for Christmas. That following Christmas, as I looked through my presents, that very same book bag was one of them.

My grandmother lived in an apartment at 1786 Amsterdam Avenue. She lived there with my cousin Bobby Phillips and John Dill who was actually my stepmother, Syvilla Fort's brother, but since him and Bobby were almost exactly the same age (they were seven years older than I was) we all considered each other cousins. Not long after my grandmother's visit, for the next couple of years I began spending almost every weekend at her house. Her daughter, my Aunt Ida who was also Bobby's mother, lived in the next apartment house with her husband and her other children, Bobby's younger siblings, his sisters Jackie and Stephanie and his brothers Jan, Gregory and Andrew. I had a very good relationship with my Aunt Ida and all my cousins and we would spend a lot of time together, especially at a particular time when we were adults. But unfortunately my grandmother and I never bonded.

All of my cousins called my grandmother "Motherdear", **but I called both my mother and my mother's Aunt Edith "Mom", so I didn't need to call a third woman "Motherdear". And the reality was, she was not a warm, nurturing person, so I called her grandma, but that got us started on the wrong foot from almost the beginning. Secondly, my grandmother had two daughters and one son, her oldest daughter who was Jean's mother, died probably before I was born, and her other daughter, my Aunt Ida, and her only son my father, and my father was clearly her favorite. The first of the half a dozen or so times I remember seeing my father was at her home and the only person my grandmother felt jealous of was me.**

One Christmas Eve, my father brought my Christmas presents to my grandmother's home while I was there. It was around 11 PM Christmas Eve, but I asked him could I open the presents? My grandmother quickly interjected, you can open them in the morning. This may have been the first time that my father and I were together around Christmas time, in any event, he looked at me and smiled and told me I could open every present. I am just glad that my grandmother did not have a heart attack.

My father was not just my grandmother's favorite; he was the celebrity of his family. I'm not certain where or how he received his initial tap dance training, but he was working as a professional tap dancer by the age of 18. Then during World War II, he was drafted on June 9, 1943, and he was placed in the Special Service Division where he entertained other soldiers until he was honorably discharged on Nov. 9, 1945, eleven months before I was born. I was one of the first "Baby Boomers".

Then using the G.I. Bill, he took courses to learn the administrative and management aspect of show business, with the American Theater Wing Professional Training Program, located at 730 Fifth Ave. in New York City.

- First course from Sept. 15, 1948 to Nov. 22, 1948
- Second course from June 20, 1949 to Nov. 22, 1949
- Third course from March 13, 1950 to May 20, 1950

Then he was drafted a second time during the Korean War on Sept. 25, 1950 and was wounded twice before being honorably discharged again on Sept. 2, 1951.

In addition to being a tap dancer and theatrical promoter he had also married a second time to Syvilla Fort, who was also a dancer who danced in the Katherine Dunham Dance Company and was eventually promoted to the Dance Director of her school (but I will cover this in more detail in chapter four).

So my father was both the shining light and patriarch of the Phillips family during the 1950's, and my grandmother could not imagine sharing her special place with anyone. As I said before, my two cousins, Bobby and Johnny lived with my grandmother and if they did anything wrong she would tell my father and he would discipline them (old school style). And he disciplined one of them once when I was their and I could hear it from a different room. Then one day my grandmother tried to force me to eat something I hated and she sent me into a bedroom with my food and told me not to come out until after I had finished eating it. There were only a few foods that I hated and I was not usually forced to eat them. So I raked the food under a bed and my grandmother found it and she told me Buddy is coming to the house, with an expression on her face that said "I got you now".

When my father came I was waiting in the bedroom, the same bedroom my cousin had received the beating, which I had heard. My grandmother told my father what I had done and he came into the bedroom. I was scared to death. He asked me why I did what I did and I told him. He told me I should not do that again and it was at that moment that I knew how much he loved me. I stopped going to my grandmother's house on the weekends and I didn't see either of them again for almost ten years.

Dad and Sonny

My dad was a very capable person; especially considering that he only had a third grade education and had been on his own since he was thirteen. My brother Sonny, even though he was only three years and eight months older than I was, he was always much bigger, stronger and very mature for his age. Since dad had to take care of the building's fifty apartments, it wasn't long before he had Sonny working right along with him. By the age of thirteen, Sonny was both going to school and doing a days' work at the same time.

If a young person is expected to do the work of an adult, it won't be long before they want the perks that go with being an adult. Sonny was drinking wine, beer and smoking cigarettes by the time he reached his early teens.

It was also around that time Sonny realized, just like we played hookey from Sunday school, we could also sometimes play hookey from public school. There's an Islamic tradition which says "you should want for your brother what you want for yourself", which is a good philosophy if a person has good values, but if someone is misguided then it could be very problematic.

By the time that I was nine years old, Sonny had taught me how to smoke cigarettes and instead of going to school, some days we would go to a friend of his house, who's both parents worked, and we would smoke cigarettes, drink beer and play cards all day. Even though our neighborhood, consisted mainly of apartment buildings that housed middle-class Whites, two blocks away at Tremont and Morris Avenues, there was one block of two story houses where Black people lived and this is often where Sonny and I would spend a lot of our free time. Sonny was very proud of his cool little brother and I was very proud of him. However, it wasn't long before I began seeing a sadness in Sonny that you usually don't see in a boy his age.

My Home Life Until I Reached My Teens

My life has always been filled with contrasts. To begin with I was born in a very small town and then at three months old I moved to New York City, one of the largest cities in the world at that time. When I say I was born in a small town, let me be a little more descriptive. There was one general store in the town and the Greyhound Bus did not stop in my town at all. If you wanted to go somewhere on the bus, the Greyhound Bus did stop in the next largest town which was twenty miles away.

Point number two, I was breast fed for the first two years of my life, you might say that my mother and I were un-separable, and then two years later my mother and I were living in two different states. Point number three, at four years old, almost every day for a year or two, I had Kosher lunches and Soul Food dinners. And my fourth and final point, which is the main point that I want to focus on in my conclusion to chapter one, was the contrast between my having been a man-child during the day but a little kid at night.

When I was in the third grade I would hang out with Sonny occasionally but usually I was with my own friends who were other kids who were around the same age as I was. It's not like I was playing hookey, drinking beer and smoking cigarettes all day every day. May be every other week we would play hookey together and I would sip on a half a glass of beer all day and smoke one or two cigarettes. They were not habits of mine; I was just being cool on those days. However, whatever I did in the street, I kept it in the street, and when I walked into the house I acted my age.

Dad belonged to the Elk's Lodge, a black branch of the Freemasons. There was a picture of him in the living room and he was wearing a tuxedo and a Moroccan Fez hat. He was proud of that picture, that picture symbolized a man who was in control of his life and part of being in control of his life meant he was also in control of his home. But after each work day was done, he would always go out and not come home until very late at night.

When I was nine, Sonny was thirteen and my cousin Edie was sixteen. I had to be in the house before dark but both Sonny and Edie would stay out very late, usually coming home after I was asleep. Usually it was only mom and I who were home in the early evenings, and she always went to bed very early. But that was alright with me because I had my good friend the television. Today there is a lot of concern because of the violence and sex that are on the television, especially the cable channels. But during the middle 1950's we only had ABC, CBS and NBC and TV programs were squeaky clean. Life was very different then, in some ways they were better and in some ways they were worse, however the fact still remains, TV programs did not portray reality.

After my mother remarried, she would always come to visit us in New York at least once a year and at some point Sonny and I began visiting her in Philadelphia at least once a year. Then one day when I was twelve, and I guess Sonny was tired of working and going to school, because he decided to move to Philadelphia. Then around six months later I decided to move to Philadelphia also.

Chapter 2
My Second Hijrah/Second Chance

My New Environment/Kids On The Block

Contrast number five, in New York I had always been the youngest child in the house, the baby, but in Philadelphia, I already had my younger brother Wakil, and three younger sisters, Ella, Francine and Lorraine, and my sister Gail was born a month after I moved there.

Contrast number six, moving from a white neighborhood in the Bronx too South Philadelphia or the Hood. Some of my classmates in the Bronx thought I was tough, but in South Philly you had some "real" tough guys. I moved to Philly in June of 1959 at the beginning of the summer vacation. My mother and stepfather had just bought a five bedroom house on 15th Street, right off of Ellsworth Street, 1122 South 15th Street to be exact. My family would live in that house for the next fifty years. However, for the next two months my world consisted of four blocks: the block that I lived on and the three intersecting blocks. This is noteworthy because in New York my friends and I would go to shows at the world famous Apollo Theater or take a one and a half hour subway ride to Coney Island on any given summer day, but at 12 years old in Philadelphia, it was as if I was going through my second childhood.

Another important point that needs to be made is that my new four block world was a black working/middle class neighborhood, but three blocks away on 16th and Federal Street, you were in the heart of the hood. Our family was the only family with kids that lived on the block and there were even two white families but they moved out not long after we moved in. On the other side of the street was a Marine Corp. factory which a couple of decades later would be converted into coop-apartments.

On the next block, 15th Street on the other side of Ellsworth Street, you had many families with children and one outstanding family was the Houston's. Mr. Houston had already passed away, so it was Mrs. Houston and her older son Mickey, the neighborhood philosopher, and her younger son Shakur Abdur-Rashid (this was not his given name, it was the name he took 15 years later when he converted to Islam). Mickey was probably around six years older than I was and was either the first or second black youth, from the neighborhood, to go to college. Mickey loved to talk and on warm summer nights he would sit on his steps for hours and talk to anyone who walked by and felt like talking. During the 1960's, Mickey and I had many long stimulating conversations sitting on his steps. Mickey's younger brother Shakur was two years younger than I was and we also became close friends and we still are to this very day. Both Mickey and Shakur eventually graduated from college but that was all they had in common. Mickey loved to talk and was very ambitious and outgoing and Shakur was quiet and introverted, and may be that's why Shakur and I became close friends because I have been known to talk a lot and he was a good listener.

It is not just a coincidence that Wilt Chamberlain came from Philadelphia; there are two main activities that young black boys in Philadelphia would do a lot of the time and one of them was playing basketball. Around the corner from my house on Ellsworth St. between Broad St. and 15th St. was the Saint Rita's Catholic School and it had a full basketball court in the back of the school. So during the day it was a Catholic school but in the afternoon the basketball court became the neighborhood playground.

Leonard: A Positive Role Model:

Around the corner from my house in the other direction, on Ellsworth St. between 15th and 16th Street there was a second outstanding family, the Green's. The Green's consisted of Mr. and Mrs. Green and there three sons and four daughters. Raymond, their oldest boy, was the other black youth who was either the first or second to go to college from the neighborhood. Mickey and Raymond were around the same age but I knew Mickey better because it seemed like Raymond was always away at college and after he graduated I think he moved to Baltimore and became a math teacher.

If Mickey was the community philosopher, then Leonard, Raymond's younger brother, was the community youth coordinator, and Leonard and I also became close friends. Some afternoons Leonard would organize/play in some of the neighborhood basketball games, and some evenings, we would play chess. Some evenings we would play two or three games and he would beat me game after game after game. Then one evening I won my first game and he said let's play another game but I said "no way". I wanted to savor my victory for as long as I could.

Even though we lived in South Philadelphia, Leonard went to West Philadelphia High School because it was a better school then. Leonard graduated from high school the same year I graduated from junior high school and he convinced me to go to West Philadelphia High School. I went to West Philly High for a year but was then transferred to South Philadelphia High. Leonard eventually graduated from law school and now has his own law practice in Philadelphia. However, the single act that Leonard did that had the most impact on my life was in the late 1960's when he gave me "The Autobiography of Malcolm X" and told me that I had to read it.

Mickey the neighborhood philosopher and Leonard the neighborhood youth coordinator shared a number of the same qualities: they were both intelligent, they were both studious but a third quality they shared that you do not always find in people who have the first two, was that they could both fight. Just like it wasn't a coincidence that Wilt Chamberlain came from Philadelphia, it also wasn't just a coincidence that "Smokin" Joe Frazier, one of the best heavy weight fighters in the history of boxing, also came from Philly.

So the other main activity that young black boys in Philly used to do was boxing. You would either slap to the head or punch to the body. Slapping to the head meant you could hit the person in the head as hard as you could as long as you kept your hands open. And punching to the body meant you could punch a person as hard as you could, with a closed fist, as long as you didn't punch him in the head. There was a little skinny boy who lived across the street from the Houston family and everyone called him "Little Jimmy". Little Jimmy and I was around the same age and I was a skinny little kid too, but Little Jimmy was an inch or two shorter than I was. But the first time that Little Jimmy and I boxed (punching to the body), I got the surprise of my life because there is no way that I can convey to you how much his boney fists hurt. After boxing with Little Jimmy, I thought to myself, what did I get myself into because in a month or so I would be starting at Barrett Junior High School where there were "real" tough guys like Buddy Dawson, the older brother of Lonnie Dawson, who would eventually become one of the leaders of Philadelphia's notorious Black Mafia until 1975 when he was convicted and given a life sentence for Murder.

In a final note concerning Little Jimmy, around ten years ago I saw a friend from the old neighborhood and he told me Little Jimmy was in prison. He also mentioned that Little Jimmy never went to prison in the 70's or 80's when many black men from the old neighborhood was going to prison. Little Jimmy didn't go to prison until he was in his fifties, and my brother Wakil told me recently that Little Jimmie is still in prison.

Chapter 3

Adolescence, Death and Love

Sonny, Adolescence and Adulthood

A few months after my moving to Philadelphia I started attending Barrett Junior High school and my brother Sonny was attending Benjamin Franklin High school. Sonny had no intention of graduating from high school, he was just waiting until he turned seventeen and then he planned to join the army. Sonny played hooky from school in Philadelphia also but Philly was less tolerant than New York City was, so the Philadelphia school system transferred Sonny to Daniel Boone High school an all boy disciplinary school where most of the students were there because they had been kicked out of their previous schools for fighting.

So Sonny decided to move back to New York. Mom and dad had not wanted me to move from the Bronx to Philly but I insisted mainly because Sonny had moved there. Now, less than a year later, Sonny was moving back to New York, but my pride would not let me move back with him. And besides, in four or five months he would be turning seventeen and joining the army, at least that is what we all thought, but unfortunately for Sonny, he never did get to join the army.

Around a month before Sonny turned seventeen, he was arrested for burglary. He was eventually convicted and given a one to five year sentence. The first time dad and I went to visit Sonny, he was in the Elmira Correctional Facility, in Elmira, New York. Decades later, having been hired as a Muslim Chaplain by the New York State, Department of Correctional Services (DOCS), Rev. Moore, the Assistant Commissioner of DOCS Ministerial Services, would call me on a Saturday morning, during the Islamic month of Ramadan, and request that I go to the Elmira Correctional Facility to help resolve a problem the facility staff was having with the Muslim inmates. During my visit to see my brother Sonny, there is no way anyone would have been able to convince me that I would one day be a chaplain, and working for the New York State Department of Correctional Services. Man plans and God plans, and God is the best of planners.

My Father Dies

During the summer of 1963, I was visiting my mom and dad in the Bronx and my cousin Bobby called me and told me my father's health was bad and that I should go to their dance studio and visit him. Bobby had taken me to the dance studio once when I was a young child but I didn't remember exactly where it was. So Bobby gave me the address, 153 West 44th Street in Manhattan, and I went to the studio. When I arrived he wasn't there but my stepmother Syvilla told me he was in their hotel room which was in the same block. So I went to his hotel room and I looked at him and he was just skin and bones, nothing like the strong, healthy man I had last seen at my grandmother's home.

This was a month or two before my 17th birthday, and he said to me he wished he had done more for me, but it appears as though I had grown into a fine young man.

We talked a little longer and then I left and went back to Philadelphia and two months later, on October 28, 1963, my father died.

Kissandra (Kissi) – My First Love

In addition to basketball and boxing, there were two other activities that young Black Philadelphians, both male and female, enjoyed doing that was wearing nice clothes and partying. Usually on Friday and Saturday nights, Black teenagers who were part of the "in crowd", would get dressed up and either go to a house party or to a dance at a ballroom or both. I was fortunate to live in South Philadelphia, because in South Philly we had the "Times Auditorium" ballroom which had at least one dance every week, and young Black males and females from every part of Philadelphia would come to the dances at "Times Auditorium".

It was at one of these dances, maybe on New Years Eve but I'm not certain, I saw this short, dark skinned beautiful young girl with dimples and a smile so warm it could melt butter. I asked her to dance, we danced and after the dance we talked. She told me her name was Kissandra but that everyone called her Kissi. She gave me her phone number and told me she lived on 11th Street and Gerard Avenue, in the Richard Allen housing projects. In other words, she lived two blocks from 12th and Popular Street, the hang-out spot for a notorious North Philadelphia gang! Needless to say, they did not like guys from other neighborhoods, coming to see the girls in their neighborhood, but as far as I was concerned, Kissi was worth taking the risk.

Kissi and I hit it off immediately, maybe because our early lives had been so different. I was a young man of the world who had lived in New York City for twelve years before moving to Philly, and I still went back to New York 3 or 4 times a year during holidays and the summer vacation. On the other hand, she had lived in the same apartment all of her life and had always attended Catholic school. Her family was not Catholic, her mother just didn't want her attending the neighborhood public schools. I was a year older than Kissi and I was in the eleventh grade and she was in the tenth. The dance where we met may have been the first dance she had ever went to.

Another way in which we differed was, me being part of the "in crowd" meant it was almost mandatory for me to attend a dance or house party every weekend, but I was actually an introvert even though I did not know that at the time, so I felt more comfortable spending the evening with whoever my girlfriend was at that time. I would visit Kissi one night every weekend and go out partying on the other night. This was good for the initial year of our relationship, but even during that year I could see signs that Kissi was like a butterfly waiting to bust out of her cocoon.

Kissi lived with her mother and two older brothers, her father had passed away some years earlier and she also had an older sister who was already married and lived in the neighborhood.

Her mother and brothers liked me because they saw me as a step above the local young thugs of the neighborhood. When I visited Kissi I might see her brothers when I first arrived but if so they would always be on their way out. Usually it would be me, Kissi and her mother in the apartment. Kissi and I would be in the living room and her mother would usually be in her bedroom. We would be alone most of the night but we knew that her mother might would come into the room at any moment so all we would do is talk and kiss.

Then one day we were talking on the telephone and Kissi told me she was not going to school the next day and that she would be home alone. I said "wonderful", I'll come and keep you company. We spent the whole day together, and we took our relationship to the next level. We would have an "on and off" relationship for the next ten years that would eventually culminate in marriage and then divorce. At times during that ten year period I had other girlfriends and she had other boyfriends but we were always there for each other in times of need.

Sonny's Young Life Comes to an End

While Sonny was incarcerated, I graduated from high school and joined the army. Sonny served three years and was then paroled, I was stationed in Germany when he was paroled, so I took a 30 day leave and came home but Sonny was not the same person, prison had changed him. He was only in his early twenties but he looked as though the world had already defeated him, the look I had seen in Black men who were much older than he was. After my 30 day leave I had to go back to Germany and Sonny violated his parole and went back to prison.

Early in February of 1968 I had returned from Germany and was at Fort Dix in New Jersey waiting to be discharged. Sonny was living in New York with mom and dad and it was a week before his twenty-fifth birthday, so I had planned on going to New York after I was discharged and giving Sonny a small party for his birthday. Then I was informed by an army official that my discharge would be expedited because they had been contacted by the Red Cross and I was informed that Sonny's body had been found in the hallway of a Harlem apartment building. He had died from an overdose of heroin and that it was necessary for me to go to the Bellevue hospital's morgue to identify the body. The man I saw in the morgue looked terrible, but it was my brother Sonny. I identified the body and funeral arrangements were made. My mother, stepfather and all my siblings came from Philadelphia for the funeral. At the viewing we all cried, but the undertaker had done an excellent job, Sonny did not look like the man I had seen in the morgue.

Chapter 4
My Third Hijrah/Back To New York City

My Stepmother – Syvilla Fort

Living in Philadelphia in 1969, I found myself in a continuous state of frustration because I was looking for something and didn't know what it was but I knew I wasn't going to find it in Philadelphia, so I moved back to New York. It was now okay for Black to be Beautiful and for someone to be proud of their African Ancestry, but for me, for get about not knowing what African country my ancestors came from, at that point in my life I knew very little about my own father.

He was no longer alive so I couldn't talk to him directly and get to know him better, but his second wife, Syvilla Fort, was still alive and we ended up becoming very close. Her and my father never had any children of their own, so to a certain extent, I became the son that her and my father never produced. Syvilla still had her dance studio at

153 West 44th Street and I found myself spending a consid-erable amount of time there. There were always some at-tractive young women at the studio, and my cousin Johnny and other drummers would play the drums for the Modern Afro-Technique dance classes. Some of the drummers gave me drumming lessons and eventually I began playing, back-ing up the professional drummers during class.

Sometimes after the last class of the night, Syvilla and I would go across the street to her studio apartment and she would cook me my favorite meal, Burgers and French Fries and we would talk for hours. During our conversations I learned a lot about my father but I also learned a lot about her and I could see what my father had seen in her.

When she died; Jet Magazine said, "The unassuming dance studio in Manhattan which has nurtured Black dance artists for the past 20 years will no longer be graced by the dynamic artistry of Syvilla Fort". The New York Times said, ".....as a teacher, Miss Fort provided a spiritual home, to-gether with training and inspiration, for three generations of black artists". Her life included a lot of joy and happiness, but I think they were out weighed by her disappointment and frustration. Syvilla having accomplished as much as she did, some people may disagree with me, but I knew her better than most, because having been her stepson, I was one of the few people she allowed into her private world of hopes and dreams.

Syvilla was born in Seattle, Washington, in the year 1917. She was the oldest of three children, John her youngest brother, eventually moved to New York with her and be-came a drummer and was with her during most of her years in New York, but in the early 1970's, he moved to Sweden so he was not with her during her final years. Syvilla always described her family as having been lower middle-class. Her father was only a postal clerk but in those days that was an extremely good job for a Black man. Syvilla lead a very orderly early life, she attended regular school during the week and would take music lessons and go to the movies on Saturdays.

Her having acquired a strong desire to become a dancer at an early age may have been a result of the movies she attended. In any event, whatever the main motivating factor was, it resulted in being her first major cause of frustration.

I had always thought that Syvilla's unique Modern-Afro Dance Technique, was the technique that maintained first place in her heart. However, to my surprise, not long before her death, I found out that she had initially wanted to be a ballet dancer and that she was denied entrance into Seattles' ballet schools, because of the fact that she was black. Her mother did eventually find her a ballet tutor but learning ballet only added to her frustration because then there were no jobs for black ballet dancers.

After having attended the Cornish School of the Arts, Syvilla moved to New York where she became a member of the Katherine Dunham Dance Company and during this time she appeared in many dance concerts and the film "Stormy Weather". Miss Dunham realizing Syvilla's talent made her the school's Dance Director; she kept this position from 1948 until she opened her own school in 1955.

It was while Syvilla was working at the Dunham School that she met my father. One day my father visited the Dunham School and he met Syvilla. Finding her attractive and wanting to get to know her better, he invited her to a show he was performing in. She found him attractive also, so she attended the show. They were eventually married and opened the Phillips-Fort Dance Studio at 153 West 44th Street, between Broadway and Sixth Avenue.

The Phillips-Fort Dance Studio was successful in every way except financially. Talented students were never turned away. If a student was long on talent and short on finances, there was always a scholarship available. In addition to their generosity, my father was wounded in the Korean War and complications from the injury began acting up, in the middle 1950's, so for the next five or six years my father was in and out of the hospital. His condition continued to worsen until he passed away in 1963.

In spite of the fact that Syvilla had to deal with the loss of her husband, the tragedy created the opportunity and necessity for Syvilla to exercise her excellent administrative abilities. The studio continued to produce at least one show each year, in addition to the musicians and dance teachers that had to be paid for the regular classes and of course there was always the rent and other expenses that had to be paid.

A number of people had suggested that she should move the studio from the downtown Broadway area and follow the example of some of her more successful students like: Chuck Davis, Arthur Mitchell and Rod Rogers. They had all began dance studios in communities where expenses were much more reasonable and they all developed successful dance companies. But to Syvilla this was out of the question; even though she had been a victim of racism, not only was she against racism, she was the strongest advocate for the advancement of racial integration that I have ever known.

In the news media she was usually described as a dance teacher who inspired Blacks or a noted Black Dance Pioneer, but sometimes she had more white students than blacks, and even though the white students did not usually do as well in the field of dance, they often did very well in other areas of the arts: Marlon Brando, James Dean, Jane Fonda and Shirley MacLaine are some of Syvilla's most famous dance students.

Syvilla was determined to keep the studio where it was as long as it was humanly possible, but my father's funeral had left Syvilla in a lot of debt and the situation did not look good. However, fortunately for her, the government of the African country of Guinea chose Harry Belafonte to organize a group to help them develop a national dance company. Harry Belafonte was a good friend and his wife Julie was an old student of Syvilla, so needless to say, Syvilla was on her way to Africa. Syvilla had made arrangements so the school could be kept open while she was away and she figured with the two incomes it would be enough to get her out of debt. Unfortunately the people she left in charge did not have the administrative ability that she had, so when she returned to New York, she found that she was no better off than before she had left. The studio had already seen its best days but through an occasional grant and Syvilla teaching dance part-time at Columbia University, she managed to keep both her and the studio going.

I think it was the early part of 1973 that Syvilla began to express that she was worried about her health. She would make appointments to see a doctor but I didn't think that she was keeping the appointments. Her close friends and I all volunteered to go to the doctor's office with her, but she always refused saying she preferred to go alone. A year later it became obvious that she had not gone to see a doctor because she was then in the hospital with a serious case of cancer. Up until 1973, she had gained some weight and was relatively heavy, but after she was admitted to the hospital she began to rapidly lose weight. I had doubts about whether she would ever leave the hospital alive.

Then sitting at home one Saturday morning, the phone rang and to my surprise it was Syvilla and she was calling from home. She informed me that some of her old students were in the musical "The Wiz", and had given her some tickets and she asked if I wanted to see it. When I replied in the affirmative, she told me to meet her at the Majestic Theatre. I arrived there before she did, and after waiting for a short time I saw Syvilla walking toward the theatre the same way I had seen her so many times in the past.

Over the next six months, she was in and out of the hospital on several occasions and each time she lost more weight, but every time I saw her, she seemed to be in good spirits. Then that October her condition took a serious turn for the worst. The Black Theatre Alliance had organized a benefit for her entitled, <u>Dance Genesis: Three Generations Salute Syvilla Fort</u>; Ironically it was to be held at the Majestic Theatre and one of the groups that was to perform there was the cast of "The Wiz". By this time her condition was so bad we did not know if she would live to see her own benefit! But thanks to the Grace of God, on the day of the benefit she was well enough to leave the hospital.

On November 3, 1975, I found myself again with Syvilla at the Majestic Theatre but this time she was the Guest of Honor and everyone was paying tribute to her. She thoroughly enjoyed herself and after the program was over she spent the night in her dance studio. However, five days later in Sloan-Kettering Hospital, Syvilla Fort's long hard event filled life, came to an end.

Before Syvilla became aware of her illness, she gave me a lot of my father's personal papers and it was through those papers and my conversations with Syvilla, that I finally began to know and understand the man my father was.

I Became A Poet

One morning I woke up around two AM and I wrote a poem, and over the next few years I would write quite a few poems and eventually publish a book of poems. In the introduction of that book I said the following:

The contents of this book are exactly what the title says: life as I see it.

I describe the affects different events, and individuals have had upon me, and in my poetry, I try to express my hopes, dreams and fears.

So in chapter five of this book you will find what I consider to be the ten best poems of my previous book. They are not in the order I wrote them but hopefully their order will give you an idea of the evolution of my thought process.

I think that it is reasonable to say that most people want to live an enjoyable life, but what each person considers acceptable, depends on their value system, what they consider to be important or valuable. Most people would probably agree on some things: a comfortable home, good food, some nice clothes, a good car, but at what cost? The white authors of our constitution considered it acceptable to enslave black people in their pursuit of happiness. And if you study world history, this type of thinking was not a uniquely American phenomenon, so the first poem I chose was "The Human Race". Then I went from my macro to my micro world view with my poem "I Want To Live".

Remember those poems were written in the early 1970's while the Viet Nam war was still going on. In 1968 Nixon said he needs to be elected president so he could end the war, but at the end of his first term, the war was still going on.

I served in the army from 1965 until 1968. After my enlistment, I was given the serial number #13856380 and forty-eight years later I still remember that number because for three years, as far as the army was concerned, that number was me. But by the Grace of God, the computer decided to send that number to Germany instead of sending it to Viet Nam. When I was honorably discharged in 1968, there was over a half a million American soldiers in Viet Nam and over 50,000 would die there, which inspired my poem "The Plea of An Unknown Soldier".

On college campuses all over America, especially in the south, there was a new black awareness, but in the poor black communities, very little had changed. Most black men and women were struggling to survive, and didn't have time to read books on Black History and political theory, so I wrote the poem "Awaken Black People Awaken". Going from macro to micro again, my next poem was inspired by my brother Sonny. Most drug addicts are manipulative criminals who would do anything for a dollar, but some like my brother Sonny, were just week individuals who were victims of their environment, as I indicated in my poem "Help! I'm A Junkie".

Gil Scott-Heron became well known after he released an album with one of his poems having been put to music. The poem was entitled "The Revolution Will Not Be Televised". However, not long after that, Hollywood began putting out black exploitation movies about black revolutionaries. These movies did not portray the warm relationship that should have existed between the black revolutionary and his woman, so my response to that was my poem "A Love Letter From A Black Revolutionary". At this point I want to make one thing clear, I was not a revolutionary militant, I was a revolutionary poet. I considered it my job to inform and educate. I would go around New York and New Jersey reading my poems, or in other words, planting philosophical seeds. Only God knows if any of those seeds bore fruit.

My brother Sonny died a week before his twenty-fifth birthday, but on my twenty-fifth birthday I moved into an air conditioned studio apartment on 83rd Street between First and Second Avenues. Sitting in my comfortable apartment and reflecting on the fact, at twenty-five years of age, I had already lived longer than my older brother, so I wrote the poem "Where Are You Now Brother".

As the 1970's progressed, J. Edgar Hoover and the FBI declared war on all black militant groups, especially their leaders, and they began to either kill them or imprison them, sometimes legally and sometimes illegally. It's true these groups advocated the violent overthrow of the American Government, they considered themselves the vanguard but expected the black masses to eventually follow them. Looking back on those days, it now seems ludicrous, but some believed that any black man that read Malcolm's autobiography and Lerone Bennett's "Before The Mayflower", should not feel comfortable dying a natural death. So I wrote the poem, "Why Am I Alive". Not only was the revolutionary leaders being killed or imprisoned in real life, on the movie screens they had been replaced by "Superfly", so I wrote the poem, "The Revolution Done Gone".

At this point, by the Grace of God, I began to realize that it was not within my ability to change the world, but it was possible for me to change myself. Americans are expected to be consumers. They are not expected to think, they are expected to follow instructions and consume. So I put the world on notice, informing them that I was going to begin thinking for myself and I wrote the poem "I Don't Have The Time".

Me and Kissi's Final Chapter

During the summer of 1972, God decided to change my life. I began throwing up all the food I ate. After doing this for two or three days, I decided to go back to Philadelphia to be with my family and seek medical attention. The problem was not obvious so a doctor gave me a thorough examination and some medication and gave me an appointment to come back in a few days to discuss the results. During the next couple of days I began experiencing severe stomach pains and after not having prayed in six years, I fell to my knees and begged God to help me. The pain became less severe immediately. At that point I knew that I had to add a spiritual dimension to my life.

When I went back to the hospital a doctor told me they didn't find anything wrong with me but it appeared as though I had a nervous stomach and I should eat only one meat meal a day. The physical pain having subsided and now knowing that there was no serious medical problem I felt the need for female companionship. I called Kissi and told her my condition and she said come on over. So I spent two or three days at Kissi's house before going back to New York.

At some point during the next year, I got a call from Kissi and she was having some personal problems and she wanted to know if she could come and stay with me in New York for a while, and I told her she could. I actually had a girl-friend in New York who I had been seeing for a few months, she was not the most attractive girl in the world but she was intelligent and personable. She was a junior in college and intended to become a lawyer. I told her we could no longer see each other because my old girlfriend was com-ing from Philadelphia to live with me. She suggested that we could still see each other from time to time, but I told her she should find a young man who could appreciate her and give her the time and attention that she deserves.

Now Kissi would go with me to the cultural events where I would read my poems and she would sometimes read poems she had written. I was still seeking some type of spiritual guidance but I was not ready to make the commit-ment that it would take to be a Muslim but I was meeting and getting more exposure to Sunni Muslims. After around six months, Kissi expressed a desire for us to get married. Spiritually it made sense, if we were going to continue to live together, we should get married. So Kissi and I went to the Justice of the Peace, with my stepmother Syvilla as our witness, and we were married.

For the next six months everything was okay, but as I got more exposure to Sunni Muslims and learned more about the religion of Islam my life began to change. I had stopped smoking cigarettes in 1969, but as I progressed spiritually, I stopped drinking alcoholic beverages, smok-ing marijuana and eating pork. Kissi continued smoke cigarettes in the house (in 1973 people did not know the danger of second hand smoke), but would not bring alcoholic beverages, marijuana or pork in the house. However, since we both used to indulge in those things together, she felt that just because I was moving toward the religion of Islam, that did not mean she should have to totally change her life.

We finally reached a point where it became obvious that we were going in two different directions. Then came the straw that broke the camels back, she said she could not have children. So I suggested that we get a divorce and I went to my mom's apartment in the Bronx and stayed there until I was able to get my own place. Six months later I took my shahadah and became a practicing Muslim. Then a year and a half later, we were legally divorced and I have never seen or heard from her since then.

Chapter 5

My Pre-Shahadah Poems

THE HUMAN RACE

*This world is a hell of a
Place
Just because of the Human
Race*

*People are being put to
Death
With every new born
Breath*

*There are millions in their
Graves
Because they didn't want
To be slaves*

*If it wasn't so serious it would
Almost seem funny
What some people will do for
That paper we call money*

*Things can be changed but it
Might take a fight
We can do it today if poor
People will unite*

I WANT TO LIVE

When I wake up on a cold winter
Morning
I want to live

When I close my eyes at
Night
I want to live

When I'm hungry and don't know where
My next meal is coming from
I want to live

When I look for a job and can't
Find one
I want to live

When I'm discriminated against because
I'm Black
I want to live

When I'm exploited because
I'm poor
I want to live

When my woman tells me to move on man
Rather than try to understand
I want to live

I want to live and I'm not going
To run
One day possibly I'll have
A son

He'll have everything that I can possibly
Give and that's probably why
I want to live

PLEA OF AN UNKNOWN SOLDIER

*Please don't shoot me Yellow
Man
It's not my fault I'm here in your
Land*

*Coming here wasn't something I
Wanted to do
I was following orders just like
You*

*Other men shouldn't have the
Right
To put us here and make us
Fight*

*They would call me a coward if I
Was to turn and run
But I'd feel better if my president
Was here with a gun*

*Try to understand where I'm
Coming from
After all we both have a lot in
Common*

*Both of our families are home
Filled with fear
Both of us are poor or we
Wouldn't be here*

*Both of us have seen good friends
Die
We are both trying to kill each other
And don't know why*

I don't want to die so please try
To understand
Whether I live or die is up to you
Yellow Man

You say you're going to kill me but
Not because you want to
If the situation was in reverse, I'd
Probably kill you too

AWAKEN BLACK PEOPLE AWAKEN

Awaken Black People from your
Endless sleep
Awaken, awaken and stand on
Your feet

Awaken to the forces that have trapped
Your mind
The forces that plan to keep you
In a bind

Awaken Black Man dope is killing your
Younger brother
Yet you and your woman insist on fighting
Each other

Oh Beautiful Black Man treat your woman
As she should be treated
Love, respect and tenderness is all she
Ever needed

Oh Beautiful Black Woman your man needs
You more than ever
Your love, warmth and inspiration is what
Keeps a brother together

Get together Black People before you are
Completely overtaken
Get together my "Beautiful People",
Awaken, awaken

HELP! I'M A JUNKIE

Help! I'm a Junkie

It seems like I been high
All my life

When I was very young I would steal
Some of my mother's beer
Or my father's liquor

The beer my mother would drink
After cooking and cleaning
And taking care of her ten children and
Having only two dresses to show for it

The liquor my father would drink
After putting up with his White bosses
Insults all day and rats and roaches
All night

I knew that beer and liquor had
To be good
Because it made life for them a
Little more bearable

When I got older, my friends and I
Would chip in and buy our
Own beer

You couldn't tell us we weren't
Hip

Beer was nice stuff but after
Awhile it wasn't
Strong enough

So we graduated to wine and
That was just fine

But from there we went to Scag
And that was real bad

Help! I'm a Junkie

The tracks on my left arm
Tells the story of

My life
Each track is a different experience
Where I stopped living and
Just existed

Each track represents some of my father's
Pain or my mother's sorrow
That I inherited and didn't have the strength
To do anything about

So here I am now, not a human being
But more like a machine

Scag is my fuel and I know I'm
A fool

I'll probably never be free
Help! I'm a Junkie

LOVE LETTER FROM A BLACK REVOLUTIONARY

I haven't been spending that much
Time with you
But it hasn't been because I haven't
Wanted to

Our relationship will always
Remain the same
But there are other things that
Have to be changed

These changes haven't just
Begun
But things won't be right until
There done

We'll get things together
Somehow
Take my word it won't be
Be long now

You've worked too hard

You've worn that dress too long

You've made too many sacrifices

You've stayed by my side and
Never complained
But I felt bad just the
Same

I've always wanted you and not
Just for fun
One day I want you to bear
My son

But I want him to grow up in a
World that's free
So he won't be forced to
Think like me

WHERE ARE YOU NOW BROTHER

Where are you now brother?

Now when there are so many things that I
Would like to do for you
In return for all those things you
Did for me

Like the time you carried me home
From the zoo
Because you spent our carfare buying me
Something to eat

Or those Saturdays when you would make a
Little spending money and take me
To the movies

You would boast to all your friends that I
Was your little brother
You were almost as proud of me
As I was of you

But there were times when I would feel
Sorry for you
Because of the work that daddy made
You do

He didn't do it trying to be
Mean
He had been on his own since he
Was thirteen

Working and going to school didn't leave

You much time to think
At a very young age it had driven
You to drink

To you it didn't matter if it was beer,
Whiskey or wine
But what bothered me was you seemed
To be drinking all the time

Normally all you could afford was
Wine
And wine has the tendency to work
On the mind

Then one day I heard something that I
Prayed would not be true
Someone saw a boy in a cop car that
Looked just like you

Jail definitely stopped you from
Drinking
But it didn't do anything to help
Your thinking

Then came the day when your
Time was through
But you weren't the same person
That I once knew

You seemed to always be depressed as
Though there was no hope
So I guess it was inevitable for you to
Start taking dope

Then one day you were finally
Set free
They found you in a hallway dead
From an O.D.

I wish you were here now Brother
So we could have fun
Like we used to

I feel guilty living in my comfortable
Home
Knowing had I been the oldest
You would have written
This poem

WHY AM I ALIVE

When my mother sat
Holding the tears back
Because of the bills she had to pay
That day
And she knew there was no way

What good was I

My brother was killing himself
With dope
And I knew there was
No hope

So all I could do was watch
Him die
And at his funeral I had
To cry

What good was I

I read books written by
Black People
And discovered why we weren't
Treated equal

I became conscious
Politically
But it didn't help my
People or me

But I continued to read and tried to
Remember what I had read
Then one tragic day I heard George
Jackson was dead

What good was I

So I sit alone writing
This poem
Wondering whether to run
Or buy a gun

Whether I should end it all or
Try to survive
I hope one day I'll know the
Answer to

Why Am I alive

THE REVOLUTION DONE GONE

Go ahead Sammy Davis and sing
Your song
Why not the revolution done came
And gone

Sisters are looking good and Brothers
Are staying high
Don't try to tell them they aint
Superfly

You can smoke your reefer or
Snort your coke
But shooting scag aint no
Joke

It was beautiful to see Huey
Set free
But everyday some brother dies
From an O.D.

Angela's free and everyone's
Glad
But Mrs. Jackson must still
Feel bad

It must be very difficult for her
To have fun
It's not easy for a mother to
Lose two sons

To me things still seem the
Same
But the word revolution suppose
To mean change

If Malcolm was here what would
He say
But it really doesn't matter
Anyway

So go ahead Sammy and finish
Your song
Just like the revolution it won't
Last too long

Go ahead Black People and keep
Struggling on
Like it or not the Revolution
Done Came and Gone

I DON'T HAVE THE TIME

When I was very young I'd watch the cowboys
And cartoons on television
But now I don't have the time

I remember when I used to wait up
For Santa Claus
But now I don't have the time

When I started school I would draw,
Paint and play all day
But now I don't have the time

Even though it didn't apply to me
I used to like history
But now I don't have the time

After high school was through I
Would party till two
But now I don't have the time

Then I joined the war and didn't
Know what it was for
I thought everyone was equal but they
Wanted me to kill Yellow People

Maybe at one time I would have
Committed their crime
And I'm not just trying to make
This poem rhyme

May be one day I'll give you
The peace sign
But now I don't have the time

Chapter 6
The Darkness Before Dawn

How the Quran changed my Life:

This chapter is an article I published in the January 2004 issue of The American Muslim magazine. I didn't realize it when I started writing this book but this article was probably part of the inspiration for the book and the book is probably a more detailed elaboration of the article.

A Child Sees the World

My view of the world as a child begins with my being born into a poor African-American Protestant family. I had one older brother, two younger brothers, and six younger sisters. My family attended a Baptist church, and I attended Sunday school. We lived in New York City, and my elementary school included White, African-American, and Hispanic students.

In the early 1950's, television was introduced into my life. Television, disguised as a means of entertainment, is actually, for most people, a tool that defines their reality. There once was a weekly series entitled "Marcus Welby, M.D." Robert Young, the series' star doctor, each week received bags of mail from viewers asking him for medical advice. Since he was only an actor, why would someone ask him for medical advice? The answer is because the character he played was real to them. That program was part of White people's reality.

But the reality for African-American people, especially children, was very different. All African-American adults on television were butlers, chauffeurs, or maids. If the time period preceded the mid-1800's, they were slaves. In elementary school, every year during February we had "Negro History Week," and every year they would show us the same movie: "The Jackie Robinson Story." The movie informed us that he was the first African-American permitted to play on a major league baseball team. It also showed the verbal insults that he had to endure from White spectators who hated him for no other reason than his color. This movie, which was supposed to make African-Americans feel proud, made me a young social scientist who wanted to learn what African-Americans were supposed to have done to make White people hate us so much.

Adolescence and My Descent into Darkness

In 1959, when I was 12 years old, my family moved to Philadelphia. As children get older, their world begins to expand. I began going to an all Black junior high school and became totally convinced that Norman Rockwell's America existed only in the movies.

In the early 1960s, the civil rights movement began to get hot. If you turned on the evening news, you might see southern White police officers making their dogs attack African-American men and women because they wanted to sit and eat in a restaurant with White people. Then an incident occurred that made the situation unbearable: An African-American church was bombed and four young girls were killed. Think about it! In a Christian country, an

African-American Christian church was bombed by White Christian men. But that was before bombing a building became a terrorist act.

A new militant component was added to the civil rights movement. Young African-American men read the Autobiography of Malcolm X and began to adopt his "By Any Means Necessary" philosophy. Some young people joined the Black Panther Party instead of the National Association for the Advancement of Colored People (NAACP). Our new young leaders, among them Huey Newton, H. Rap Brown, George Jackson, and Angela Davis, were no longer satisfied with the status quo. These were difficult times, and some of us were living in a state of desperation and confusion. While in this state of mind, one day I sat down and wrote the following poem.

Why Am I Alive?

*When my mother sat holding the tears
Back*

*Because of the bills she had to pay that
Day*

And she knew there was no way.

What good was I?

*My brother was killing himself with dope
And I knew there was no hope,*

*So all I could do was watch him die,
And at his funeral I had to cry.*

What good was I?

I began reading books written by Black
People

And discovered why we weren't treated
Equal.

I became conscious politically,
But it didn't help my people or me.

But I continued to read and tried to
Remember what I had read,

Then one tragic day I heard George
Jackson was dead.

What good was I?

So I sit alone writing this poem,
Wondering whether to run or buy a gun.

Whether I should end it all or try to
Survive.

Maybe one day I'll know the answer to:

Why am I alive?

My Search for Spiritual Guidance

In spite of considering myself a social scientist, I was not a good student in either elementary or secondary school. I did very little reading, and most of my learning came through personal observation and life experiences. But in 1969, a friend gave me a copy of the Autobiography of Malcolm X and told me that I had to read it. Once I began reading this book, I could not put it down. Even though he was the most dynamic individual that I had ever heard of, at the same time he was an individual that could have lived in my neighborhood. Malcolm was intelligent, capable, committed, and totally courageous, fearing no man and not even death itself. Whatever Malcolm committed himself to, he gave it 100 percent. When he was a follower of Elijah Muhammad, leader of the Nation of Islam, he was totally committed. And when he eventually entered into true Islam, he was totally committed.

Malcolm's biography did not describe the true religion of Islam in any detail, but it did give a very powerful description of the brotherhood that he had experienced during his pilgrimage to Makkah in 1964. Obviously, for young African-American men who grew up in the US during the 1950s and 1960s, it would have a profound impact on our hearts and minds. However, I was not religious at all, at that time, nor was I looking for religion.

But I have to admit that I did entertain the thought that if I ever felt the need for religion, I would have to consider Islam. I, like most Americans, had this dual personality, just like the American Founding Fathers, who declared that all men were created equal while they owned African slaves. So, on the one hand morality and ethics were important to me, but sometimes, while pursuing worldly pleasures, morality and ethics were put on a shelf – at least temporarily.

Then I experienced a very defining moment in my life: I became sick and began throwing up all the food that I ate. After doing this for two or three days, I went to the hospital. The doctors gave me a thorough examination, and I was given an appointment to come back and find out the results. While at home, I was experiencing serious stomach pains. At one point, it almost seemed unbearable. When I was a child, I used to say my prayers every night before going to bed. However, I stopped praying at the age of 19.

So there I was at the age of 25, not having said a prayer in six years, falling to my knees and beginning to pray. I asked my Creator to forgive me and to please help me in my time of need. The pain immediately became bearable. When I returned to the hospital, the doctor informed me that he had found nothing wrong with me. The doctor's last words were: "It appears that you have a nervous stomach, and you should only eat one meat meal a day."

At that point, I knew I needed to add a spiritual element to my life. But what? I had grown pu as a Christian, and yet had no desire to return to the church. I had a certain attraction to Islam, but I was not ready to make the commitment that it would require. I had been studying and teaching martial arts on and off for six years, so I decided to study Buddhism, its spiritual aspect. The Buddhist literature that I read did not provide satisfactory answers to my questions, nor did it adequately fill the spiritual void in my heart. So I finally decided to get some books on Islam.

My Journey from the Darkness of Ignorance to the Light of Islam

In the early 1970s, I used to go to African-American community cultural activities in New York and New Jersey. I met some African-American Sunni Muslims at these activities, and they recommended some books that adequately answered my questions and convinced me that Islam was a very comprehensive and balanced way of life. Not a religion, but a way of life, which was exactly what I needed. However, in spite of this conviction, I did not have the certainty (yaqeen) that I needed to make a total commitment.

In my heart, I knew that this certainty could come only from the Quran. And so I bought a Quran. When I say I bought a Quran, I mean that I bought a Quran that included the English translation, because the Quran was revealed in Arabic and consists of the exact words of Allah conveyed to Prophet Muhammad by the Angel Jibreel (Gabriel). Since I did not know Arabic, I needed an English translation.

Here, I would like to clear up a misconception. Accepting the truth does not come from knowing Arabic; rather, it is a blessing from Allah. This is why an Arabic speaking person may be an atheist and a non-Arab person may be totally convinced that Allah is the Creator of the heavens and Earth. If a person intends to be a scholar of Islam, then he or she needs to know Arabic. However, knowing Arabic is not synonymous with having faith.

So I opened my Quran and read the first page. Then I read the Quran every day for the next two weeks, but could not get past the first page. Surat al-Fatiha, the opening chapter, had such an impact on my heart that initially I felt that it was enough for me and that I did not need to read any more. In the words of Allah, this short chapter reads as follows: "In the Name of Allah, the Beneficent, the Merciful. Praise be to Allah, the Lord of the Worlds. The Beneficent, the Merciful. Master of the Day of Judgment. You alone do we worship, and You alone do we ask for help. Guide us on the straight path. The path of those whom You have favored, not the path of those who have earned Your anger, nor of those who have gone astray" (1:1-7).

This opening prayer of the Quran seemed to be the beginning of my heart's healing process. I eventually forced myself to read the rest of the Quran and, at this point, reading it became a 28-year learning experience. I became totally convinced that my Creator was the author of the Quran, because it told me things about myself that only my Creator could know. Paradise and the Hellfire became realities for me, so I could no longer sit on the fence. I had to make a choice. So my choice was to go to the mosque and say the testimony of faith (shahadah): "I bear witness that there is nothing (and no one) worthy of worship except Allah, and I bear witness that Muhammad is the Messenger of Allah."

Chapter 7
My Post Shahadah Poems

This book is my spiritual journey from birth to my becoming a Muslim, but I have decided to include six poems I wrote after I became a Muslim. In the first six chapters I describe my life up until the time I became a Muslim and you can say that the six poems in this chapter describes my life after I became a Muslim. To begin with, from 1970 to 1974 I wrote many poems because there were many aspects of life that I did not understand which caused me a great deal of frustration and I found that writing poems was a good way of venting that frustration. However, from 1974 until the present, I have written very few poems because the religion of Islam answered all my questions, so instead of my poetry being motivated by frustration, in most cases they began being motivated by joy and hope.

I was lost and Islam gave me guidance, so I wrote the poem "Prayer of Appreciation". Never having had a real relationship with my father, I felt so blessed when my son Yusuf was born, so I wrote the poem "Ibney (my son) Yusuf". On a personal level my life was very fulfilling but one area of frustration that remained was my concern for my Muslim brothers and sisters, so I wrote the poem "Who Am I".

A Muslim community that I used to belong too put out a monthly newsletter and they asked me to contribute some type of article. This was during a time when a lot of effort was being made to get Muslims to vote. At that time it was not real important to me whether Muslims voted or not, because when it came to Muslims, I did not expect any major differences from either candidate, but it would have been politically incorrect for me to have said that, so instead I gave them the poem "Can A Leopard Change His Spots".

My son Yusuf was born when I was a college student at San Francisco State University. Then I graduated and took a job teaching at an Islamic School in Los Angeles. After a year, I took a job teaching at an Islamic school in Philadelphia. Then two years later I took a job teaching at Madrasat Al Islamiya in New York City. At that time, Islamic schools paid minimum wage or a little better, so we were living from paycheck to paycheck. But two weeks after my son Osama was born, I was hired to be a Muslim chaplain, for the New York State Department of Correctional Services and my salary tripled. When Yusuf was born it was a joy just to have a son. But in my poem "Ibney (my son) Osama", it is the reflections and aspirations of a father who had been blessed to have been able to provide a good home for his family in general, and Osama in particular.

Then I conclude the chapter by summarizing my life in my poem "Prayer of Hope".

PRAYER OF APPRECIATION

Thank you for creating me and making
Me a Muslim

Thank you for also blessing me with a wife
Who is Muslim

Thank you also for my son and please bless me
I beg Thee with more children who
Will be Muslim

When Shaitan and his family tries
To distract me
Please remind me that
I'm Muslim

And when my naffs try to lead me
Away from Thee
Again remind me that
I'm Muslim
And may me and my family
Strive for piety
Oh I beg Thee as
A Muslim

But most of all, please let my
Family, friends and me
Return to Thee
As Muslims

IBNEY YUSUF

I have spent peaceful mornings in
New York's Central Park

And have feasted in the coolness of
An Arabian dessert oasis

I have watched the sunset over the
San Francisco Bay

And I have swam in the pure waters of
The Mediterranean Sea

I have seen the Pyramids
And have sat sipping tea while
Overlooking the Nile

But none of these can compare with
The fulfillment that I get
From seeing Yusuf's loving smile

WHO AM I

My home is comfortable

My stomach is full

My pockets are full

And the graveyards are full

Full of the bodies of my
Brothers and sisters

I am angry

I am mad

But most of all I am sad

Sad because I lack the Eman that
It would take
To stop my brothers and sisters
From being killed

The disease in my heart makes me
Eat, drink and be merry
While my brothers and sisters
Are starving

Strong Eman could cure me of
My disease
But my Eman is weak so my disease
Grows stronger

Do you want to know who I am?

No! I am not an Arab

Nor am I an American, African
Or Pakistani

I am the Muslims

CAN A LEOPARD CHANGE HIS SPOTS

Maybe the beast will change, even though
He has gotten big and strong from having
Devoured numerous animals of the jungle

Maybe the beast will change, even though
His devastation has touched jungles all
Over the world

The beast should not be blamed for
Satisfying his carnivorous appetite,
After all he has to live too

Unfortunately for us, it takes so much of
Our flesh and blood to insure that he can
Continue to grow bigger and stronger

But you have to admit the beast does
Not discriminate, he devours animals
From all jungles equally

And there is no reason to stand up to him
Because he is so much bigger than we are,
And besides, we are not carnivores

So what if it is humiliating? A wise animal
Knows that he will always be humiliated
As long as he ignores the truth

Maybe if we unite we can replace the
Beast with a more humane beast
But let us never forget: a beast will never
Be anything other than a beast

IBNEY OSAMA

*It is a blessing to have a life of
Enjoyment and fun
And one of my main sources is
Osama my son*

I would walk a mile/to see his smile

I feel sad/when he feels bad

I am filled with pity/when he's not healthy

Watching him and his brother play/makes my day

And as time goes by/I'll continue to try

To prepare him for life/and a pious wife

Then Insha Allah/my work will be done

*He Insha Allah will be Muslim and have his own
pious son*

PRAYER OF HOPE

Oh Allah please never let me
Forget Thy Grace

As time goes by through success
And failure
Please never let me forget
My place

Conceived through my
Mother's pain
And it would be a shame
If it were in vain

To stray from the path
Would be insane
And I don't want to dwell
In Hell again

I have already experienced the
Fitna of earth
And I surely couldn't bear it knowing
The Hell-fire is worse

So please save me from that
Awful curse
By always reminding me that
You come first

By always reminding me that You
Are my only friend
And that after my earthly struggle
Insha Allah
Your Paradise will be my end!

Conclusion

A person performs thousands of different actions in any given day. From the time he opens his eyes in the morning, washes his face and brushes his teeth, then looking at each garment in his closet and deciding what to wear and if he should eat breakfast or not, and if so, what should he eat? He could have already performed a hundred actions and the day has just begun and he hasn't left the house yet.

If a person is going to write an autobiography, obviously he is not going to include all of his life experiences. If a person tried, it would take many volumes to document, and besides no one is interested in anyone's daily mundane experiences. So when writing an autobiography, a person carefully chooses those experiences that he considers necessary, relevant and interesting. Most writers would like to portray themselves as positively as possible, but there are no angels walking around the earth that I know of, consequently, everyone has some skeletons in their closet. With that in mind, in an effort to make one's biography realistic and objective, it would make sense for an author to include some of the good, bad and the ugly.

However, my book is not an autobiography; it is a description of my spiritual journey. I have included the biographical background that I thought was necessary and life experiences that I thought were relevant and hopefully interesting, but with much fewer details than is usually found in an autobiography. I have tried, to the best of my ability, to make the book as accurate as possible, but in the two percent of the content that is factually inconsistent, this is primarily due to my either omitting some information, or stretching the truth in an effort to avoid any unnecessary offence and/or embarrassment to family members or loved ones. Allah knows my intention, and may He include this book on my scale of good deeds, when I stand before Him, on the Day of Judgment.

Sabur Abdul-Salaam
February 26, 2013

Glossary

Coke: (slang) Cocaine

Eman: Faith

Fitna: Temptations, trials and tribulations of life

High: (slang) Intoxicated

Hijrah: Migration, move from one place and settle in another

Hip: (slang) Trendy, stylish

Hood: (slang) An inner-city minority neighborhood

Hookey: (slang) Play truant

Insha Allah: God willing

Jennat Al Ferdous: Highest level of Paradise

Junkie: (slang) A person addicted to intoxicating drugs

Naffs: One's self or desires

Reefer: (slang) Marijuana cigarettes

Scag: (slang) Heroin, addictive drug derived from morphine

Shahadah: A declaration of the Muslim faith which is said in the Arabic language and means; "I declare that there is no deity worthy of worship except God, and I declare that Muhammad is the Servant and Messenger of God.

Shaikh: A scholar or a person worthy of respect

Shooting: (slang) Injecting drugs into one's body for the purpose of getting intoxicated

Sunni: Muslims who recognize the legitimacy of the first four Caliphs in the order of their leadership

Superfly: A fictional character who was a cool drug dealer in a very popular movie of the early 1970's

Tracks: (slang) The needle marks from injecting intoxicating drugs into one's body

Made in the USA
Charleston, SC
12 March 2013